PUPPIES

Sticker Activity Book

Little Doggies

Yorkshire Terrier

West Highland White Terrier

English Bulldog

Boxer

Poodle

Pomeranian

Pug

Beagle

Jack Russell Terrier

Labrador

Daschund

Cavalier King Charles Spaniel

Chihuahua

Dalmatian

Golden Retriever

Maze

Help the Dalmatian pup to find its way through the maze.

Word search

I	X	J	Y	H	C	P	P	R	S	D	O	S	Y	K
Z	L	D	M	A	O	A	K	G	G	A	M	D	X	P
E	U	W	D	O	M	X	I	K	U	X	F	R	N	P
W	V	Q	D	F	H	P	G	H	P	S	D	H	A	R
N	A	L	O	N	M	O	A	I	C	J	I	N	H	O
O	E	J	F	D	N	U	H	C	S	A	D	P	Z	M
U	T	R	I	L	H	Q	U	O	U	Q	V	O	G	I
B	O	F	S	I	N	L	F	Y	X	Y	M	M	Y	O
J	D	F	H	A	B	J	I	X	Z	N	X	E	P	V
I	U	C	R	Q	B	B	U	C	B	J	A	R	M	C
F	D	A	L	M	A	T	I	A	N	N	S	A	J	T
S	Q	B	G	H	L	L	Q	Y	N	F	L	N	S	Z
X	V	N	A	Y	F	L	U	T	A	O	W	I	H	Y
N	P	X	Q	H	P	P	F	B	O	T	I	A	B	D
O	H	J	G	E	L	G	A	E	B	X	W	N	H	V

How many of the words from the list can you find in the grid? Cross out each word as you find it.

Daschund
Dalmatian
Chihuahua
Beagle
Poodle
Pomeranian

Can you tell?

Look at the picture closely. Can you tell...

1. What colour the puppy's ears are?

2. How many spots it has?

3. How many legs it has?

4. What colour are its eyes?

Cute Pups

Border Collie

Basset Hound

Bichon Frise

German Shepherd

Border Terrier

Maltese

St. Bernard

Shetland Sheepdog

Cocker Spaniel

Schnauzer

Schnoodle

Sharpei

Airedale Terrier

Pembroke Welsh Corgi

Staffordshire Bull Terrier

Match the following

What is each of these puppies called? Match the name to the picture.

Bichon Frise

Basset Hound

St. Bernard

Picture crossword

Identify the puppy, then write down its name in the boxes.

- 🔴 Down
- 🟡 Across

1 ¹B 2 ²B
³C   ⁴S
⁵S
⁶M ⁷S

Adorable Puppies

Spitz

Kleiner Munsterlander

Rottweiler

Dogue de Bordeaux

Bernese Mountain Dog

Greyhound

Siberian Husky

American Cocker Spaniel

Appenzeller Sennenhund

Belgian Tervuren

Australian Shepherd

Chow Chow

Alaskan Klee Kai

Cane Corso

Great Dane

Join the dots

Trace the dotted line. Then colour to complete the picture.

Word search

C	H	S	P	C	E	V	E	D	K	T	G	R	N	A
I	U	E	C	N	Z	V	D	W	Q	A	M	D	S	N
M	B	U	N	G	R	E	A	T	D	A	N	E	L	T
Y	I	J	I	L	I	E	X	T	J	T	W	R	N	G
E	E	N	Q	Y	G	B	L	N	T	O	Y	G	V	R
G	G	L	F	K	O	Q	K	I	K	Q	D	B	B	R
O	G	M	G	U	H	J	I	C	E	N	M	H	H	O
J	S	Q	T	Z	W	Z	N	U	U	W	M	C	K	A
X	W	R	M	D	D	D	J	L	O	L	A	T	X	Z	E
Z	T	X	O	X	J	T	H	I	B	A	D	T	E	S
N	O	Z	N	C	O	Y	F	M	E	F	I	T	O	Q
X	D	P	E	C	E	S	X	M	O	P	D	F	R	R
S	D	A	C	R	M	N	Y	S	S	O	O	H	V	S
A	O	G	G	S	D	I	A	F	B	S	Y	Q	C	X
M	C	S	C	C	H	O	W	C	H	O	W	S	Y	X

How many of the words from the list can you find in the grid? Cross out each word as you find it.

Greyhound
Cane Corso
Chow Chow
Great Dane
Rottweiler
Spitz

Maze

Help the little pup find its way to the bone through the maze.

Cuddly Doggies

Bearded Collie

Portuguese Water Dog

Tibetan Mastiff

Coton de Tulear

Rhodesian Ridgeback

Pekingese

Papillon

Briard

Lhasa Apso

Shikoku

Brittany Spaniel

Soft-coated Wheaten Terrier

Match the following

What is each of these puppies called? Match the name to the picture.

Papillon

Pekingese

Bearded Collie

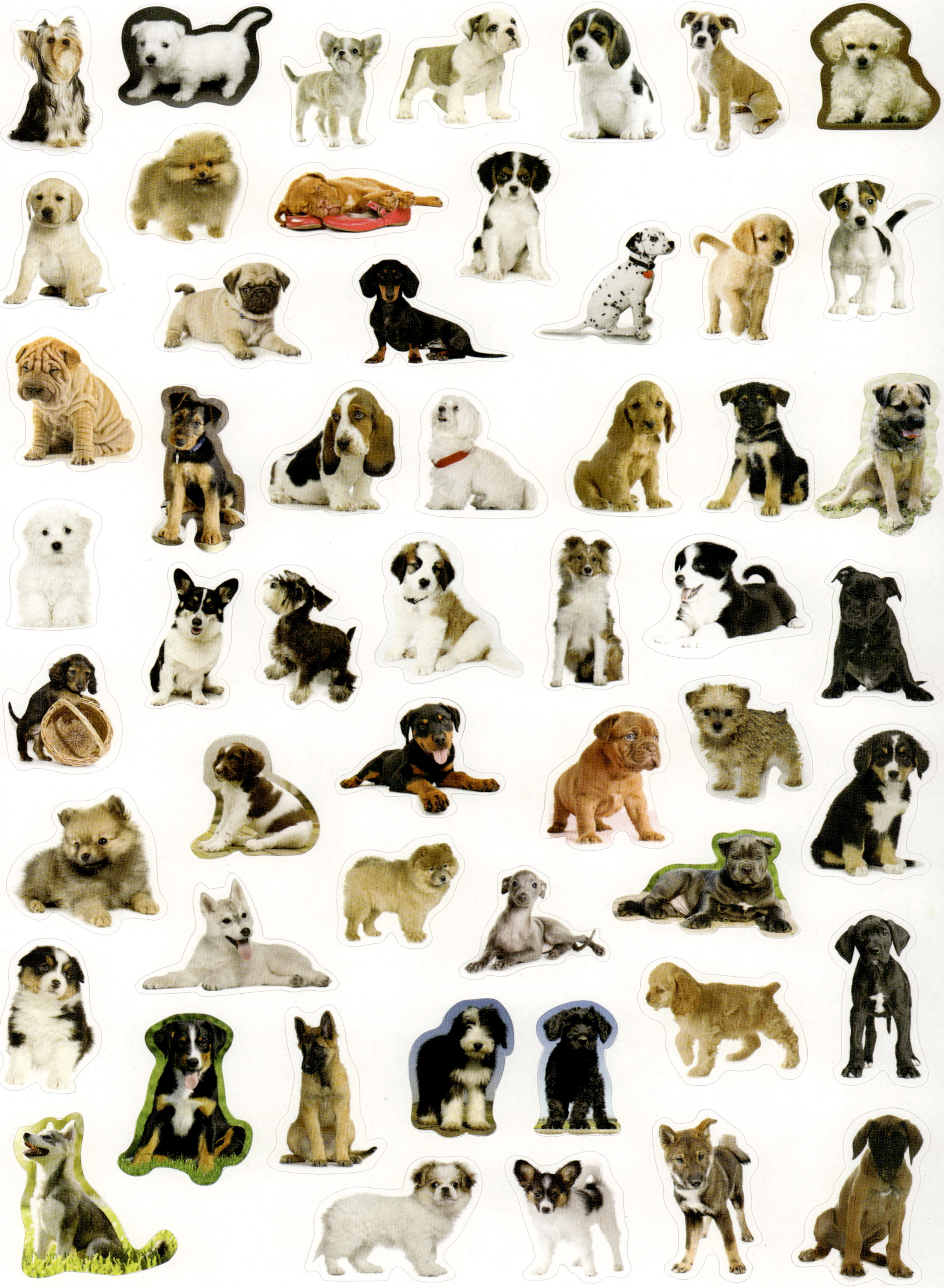

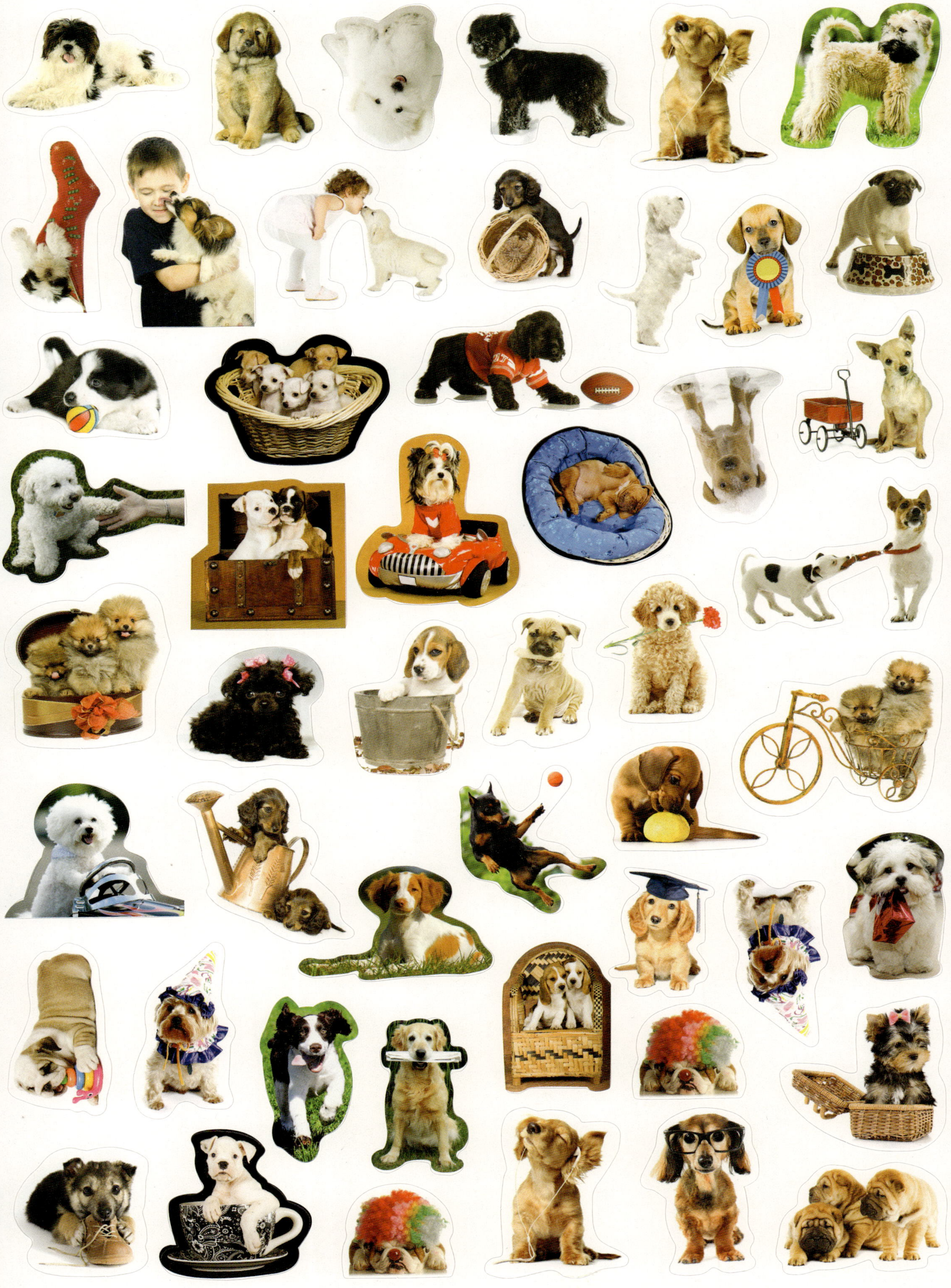

Picture crossword

Identify the pup, then write down its name in the boxes.

¹B
²B
³P
⁴P
⁵S

○ Across
○ Down

Playful Pups

Feed me!

Winner takes it all

Jumping Jack

Standing tall

Love you!

Kiss and tell

Let's play ball

Play time

Sitting pretty

Bubble bath!

Nice and chewy

Paw-shake

Brothers in a basket

Sweet dreams

Tug of war

Find the odd one out

Of these pictures, which one is not of a puppy?

Find the twins

Two of these little doggies are identical. Find them and circle them.

Maze

Help the little pug find its way to the kennel through the maze.

Being Silly

Gift-wrapped

Friends forever

Fun girl

Off we go

Flowers for my lady

Bucketful of naughtiness

Present for me!

All ears

Pretty in pink

Zooming away

What's this fruit?

Want to play?

Can you tell?

Look at the picture closely. Can you tell...

1. How many pups there are?
2. How many wheels can you see?
3. What the colour of the cycle is?

Join the dots

Trace the dotted line. Then, colour to complete the picture.

Spot the difference

There are 4 differences between the two pictures. Can you spot them all?

Fooling Around

My Christmas stocking

Running is fun

Newspaper boy

Hide and seek

We are family

The graduate

Where are the books?

Tea anyone?

Party time!

Basket case

Pink's my favourite colour

Shoes are yummy!

Clowning

On a song

Bundle of joy

Find the twins

Two of these pups look exactly the same. Find them and circle them.

Find me!

Which puppies are described here?

1. Going to a birthday party

2. At a circus

3. I love this beautiful song

4. What is in the basket?

Find the odd one out

Of these pictures, which one is not of a puppy?